INHALT

So viele Zeichen im Workbook – was bedeuten sie?

Die Ampel – Wie schwer fällt dir eine Übung?
In der Ampel kannst du markieren, wie schwer dir eine (Teil-)Übung gefallen ist:
rot = schwer, gelb = mittel, grün = leicht.

Leere und volle Kreise – jeder so gut er kann
Leichtere Aufgaben sind mit einem leeren Kreis markiert und schwierigere mit einem vollen. Die Übungen ohne spezielle Markierungen sind auf einem Niveau, das alle Schülerinnen und Schüler lösen können.

3

Kopfhörer – Audios online
Immer wenn du bei einer Übung das Kopfhörersymbol siehst, gibt es dazu Audio Tracks online. Wie du an sie herankommst. wird auf der letzten Seite erklärt. Die Zahl unter dem Kopfhörer nennt dir die Tracknummer.

5718

Das e-Workbook
Das e-Workbook bietet dir viele zusätzliche, interaktive Übungen an. Der Quickcode im Workbook verweist auf die passende Aufgabe im e-Workbook.

Stift und Partnerarbeit – wie du diese Übungen bearbeiten sollst
Für Aufgaben, neben denen ein Stift abgebildet ist, schreibst du deine Antwort auf ein anderes Blatt Papier. Die beiden Köpfe beziehen sich auf Übungen, die du mit einem Partner / mit einer Partnerin bearbeiten kannst.

Diese Arbeitsanweisungen findest du häufig im Workbook:

Act the dialogue.	*Spielt den Dialog.*
Answer the questions.	*Beantworte die Frage*
Ask your partner the questions.	*Stelle deiner Partnerin / deinem Partner die Fragen.*
Change the words in red.	*Ändere die Wörter in Rot.*
Check your answers.	*Überprüfe deine Antworten.*
Circle the right word.	*Kreise das richtige Wort ein.*
Complete the dialogue.	*Vervollständige den Dialog.*
Copy the right words.	*Schreibe die richtigen Wörter ab.*
Correct the mistakes.	*Korrigiere die Fehler.*
Cross out the wrong words.	*Streiche die falschen Wörter durch.*
Discuss these sports with a partner.	*Bespreche diese Sportarten mit deiner Partnerin / deinem Partner.*
Draw arrows.	*Zeichne Pfeile.*
Draw lines.	*Zeichne (Verbindungs-)Linien.*
Fill in the missing information.	*Ergänze die fehlenden Informationen.*
Find the right pronouns.	*Finde die richtigen Pronomen.*
Finish the sentences.	*Beende die Sätze.*
Fold the paper.	*Falte das Papier.*
Follow these instructions.	*Folge diesen Arbeitsanweisungen.*
Guess the answers.	*Errate die Antworten.*
Highlight the information.	*Markiere die Informationen.*
How do you say this in English?	*Wie sagt man das auf Englisch?*
Imagine you are the teacher.	*Stell dir vor, du bist der Lehrer / die Lehrerin.*
Label the photos.	*Beschrifte die Photos.*
Listen to the answers.	*Hör dir die Antworten an.*
Look at the picture.	*Schau dir das Bild an.*
Make a network about animals.	*Mache ein Wortnetz über Tiere.*
Mark the mistakes.	*Markiere die Fehler.*
Match the pictures with the instructions.	*Ordne die Bilder den Arbeitsanweisungen zu.*
Open the paper.	*Öffne das (Blatt) Papier.*
Pass the paper to the person on your right.	*Gib das (Blatt) Papier der Person zu deiner Rechten.*
Pick five difficult words.	*Wähle fünf schwierige Wörter aus.*
Practice the dialogue.	*Übt den Dialog.*
Put the pictures in the right order.	*Bringe die Bilder in die richtige Reihenfolge.*
Put the verbs in the simple past.	*Setze die Verben in die Vergangenheit.*
Read the emails.	*Lies die E-Mails.*
Show your email to your partner.	*Zeige deine E-Mail deiner Partnerin / deinem Partner.*
Swap roles.	*Tauscht die Rollen.*
Take an empty piece of paper.	*Nimm ein leeres Blatt Papier.*
Talk to your partner.	*Sprich mit deiner Partnerin / deinem Partner.*
Tell the story.	*Erzähle die Geschichte.*
Think of more words.	*Denke dir mehr Wörter aus.*
Tick the right answer.	*Kreuze die richtige Antwort an.*
Underline the verbs.	*Unterstreiche die Verben.*
Use the words from the box.	*Verwende die Wörter aus dem Kasten.*
Use your ideas.	*Verwende deine Ideen.*
Walk around.	*Laufe umher.*
What do you think about it?	*Was denkst du darüber?*
What's right?	*Was ist richtig?*
Which months are they?	*Welche Monate sind das?*
Work with a partner.	*Arbeite mit einer Partnerin / einem Partner.*
Write as many sentences as you can.	*Schreibe so viele Sätze wie du kannst.*
Write what they say.	*Schreibe auf, was sie sagen.*

I love London

1 What do you know about London?

a) Write the answers and find out what the word in yellow is:

1 The name for London's underground trains.
2 The Queen lives in ... Palace.
3 London taxis aren't white. They're ...
4 London's biggest football stadium.
5 You can see London very well from the London ...
6 London's most famous detective was Sherlock ...

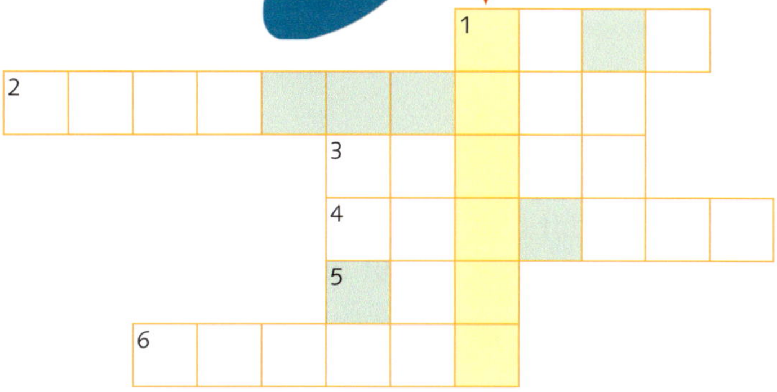

b) The word in yellow is the name of London's river. What is it?

The river ______________ .

c) Put the green letters in the right order and write the name of this famous place.

It's ______________ .

0301

▸ SB p. 9

2 More about London

a) Circle the right answers.

1 Liverpool Street is a station / hospital.
2 The Tower of London / Thames Tower is old and scary.
3 Trafalgar Market / Trafalgar Square is where people like to meet.
4 In St James's Park you can feed the cows / birds.
5 Westminster Abbey is more than 900 years old / not very old.
6 Buckingham Palace has 775 / 75 rooms.
7 Chelsea is a big London river / London football club.

b) Watch the London Tour again and check your answers.

▸ SB p. 9

3 Describing a town

a) Circle the positive ☺ words. Underline the negative ☹ words.

special dirty expensive perfect great cool amazing
friendly noisy crowded good bad boring

b) Which of the words in a) describe where you live?

0403

► SB p. 11

4 British culture

a) What do you know about British culture?
Write the words from the box in the correct list and then add some more ideas.

football • Sherlock Holmes • Buckingham Palace • Christmas • the Tube • fish and chips • uniform • cricket • Halloween • rugby • Big Ben • finishes at 3.30 p.m. • Harry Potter • muffins

Food and drink	School	Sports
scones	starts at 9am	Olympics 2012

Festivals	London	People
Guy Fawkes Night	Red buses	The Queen

0404

b) Now look at your partner's ideas and put them into your lists too.

► SB p. 11

5 Places in London

a) Do you know these places (1–6)? If you know the name, write the letter in the box.

A Covent Garden	**B** Houses of Parliament
C Trafalgar Square	**D** Piccadilly Circus
E The Shard	**F** Tower Bridge

1

2

3

4

5

6

0505

2 b) Listen and check your answers.

c) Now write the names of the places under the photos.

2 d) Listen again. Circle the right answers.

1 You can / can't visit the Houses of Parliament.

2 People like to have picnics / meet at Piccadilly Circus.

3 Covent Garden has cafes, restaurants and shops / a big market for fruit and vegetables.

4 You can visit the Shard between 9 a.m. and 6 p.m. / 10 p.m.

5 You can cross Tower Bridge only by bike or on foot[1] / by bus, by car, by bike, or on foot.

6 15 million / 50 million tourists visit Trafalgar Square every year.

You can use this information[2] for your London plans on page 13 of your Students' Book.

► *SB p. 13*

[1] on foot *zu Fuß* [2] information *Information*

6 Activities in the story

Can you complete the sentences? Use these verbs:

came • heard • kicked • left • met • ran

1 Sherlock __________ his friends last Saturday.

2 At Fulham Tube station, the friends __________ to the train.

3 When the train __________, Alfie wasn't on it.

4 Sherlock, Tally and Ruby waited ten minutes, and then the next train __________.

5 In the park, Alfie __________ the football into the teenagers' picnic.

6 The teenagers ran away when they __________ the noise of a police car.

0606

▸ SB p. 15

7 People and places in the story

Read the sentences, then write the missing words. They are all in the story.

1 People call Sam Holmes 'Sherlock' – like the famous ☐☐☐☐☐☐☐☐☐

2 Sherlock loves books, history and museums, so his friends call him a ☐☐☐☐

3 When the Tube train left, Alfie was still on the ☐☐☐☐☐☐☐☐

4 In Harrods the friends had trouble with a ☐☐☐☐☐☐☐☐ man.

5 Sherlock shouted 'Mum!' when he saw a ☐☐☐☐☐

6 In the museum the friends liked the ☐☐☐☐☐☐☐☐☐☐ room.

0607

▸ SB p. 15

8 A disaster

Tell the story. Write a sentence for each picture.

1 I wanted to ______________________________.

2 But I ______________________________.

3 I ______________________________.

4 When I got to the concert, ______________________________.

▸ SB p. 15

9 WRITING Making your article better

a) Good texts use linking words.
Read Chris's text and circle the right linking words.

Brixton

I live in Brixton, in the south of London. I like Brixton after / because it has good cinemas and lots of shops. There's a good market every day. I go to the market when / but I come back from school. The food is great and / so it's cheap. I love basketball. I sometimes play basketball at Brockwell Park. It's free, but / because it's a long way from our flat. I don't have a bike, so / after I have to travel by bus. I also go to the Brixton Road Youth Club[1]. I like it because / so there are lots of fun activities there. I like dancing, so / but I go to a dancing club with my friends. Brixton is OK, but / so I'd like more parks and cheaper buses.

Chris

0709

b) Good texts also use adjectives.
Put adjectives into these sentences to make them more interesting!

good • interesting • fun • cheap • expensive • boring • great • amazing • nice • new • old • modern • safe • busy • big • small

You can also write other adjectives!

better • bigger • nicer • cheaper

1 My neighbourhood has lots of ______________ second-hand shops.

2 There's also a ______________ park with a ______________ theatre for kids.

3 Lots of visitors come to our town. They visit the ______________ town centre.

4 They also go to the ______________ museum.

5 We're very lucky here, because there are lots of ______________ cafés and restaurants.

6 But I think we have too many ______________ shops.

7 I think we should have a ______________ sports centre here.

8 And I'd like to have a ______________ cinema.

c) NOW YOU Work with a partner.
Look again at the text you wrote about your neighbourhood from page 16 of your book.

- Did you and your partner use linking words in your texts?
  Are the linking words right? Can you write more linking words?
- Did you and your partner use good adjectives in your texts? Can you write more?

▸ SB p. 16

[1] youth club *Jugendclub*

10 READING A trip to London

a) Read the three texts. Find the right picture for each text. One picture has no text.

A

B

C

D

Buckingham Palace

Did you watch Prince William kiss his wife on the balcony of Buckingham Palace on their wedding day in 2011? Now you too can go inside the palace and see the Grand Hall, the Music Room, and other fine rooms. You can even have tea, coffee, sandwiches, cakes or scones in the garden cafe! But sorry – you won't see the Queen! You can visit Buckingham Palace from 30th June to 8th July and from 31st July to 7th October. Prices are £18 for adults, £10.25 for children under 17. Nearest Tube station: Victoria.

Picture

More London Free Festival

The 'More London Free Festival' offers free theatre, free music and free films from early July to late September.
All festival activities take place at the Scoop, London's outdoor amphitheatre next to the river, near London Bridge. Come early if you want the best seats!
For a programme and more information check on the internet.

Picture

Tooting bec Lido

Do you like swimming?
Tooting Bec Lido is the largest fresh water, open air swimming pool in England! Our 90 metre pool has been open for over 100 years.
It's open all through the year, but if you'd like to swim in winter you have to be a member of the South London Swimming Club. Tooting Bec Lido is in south London, not far from Tooting Bec Tube station.
For prices, please visit our website.
Facilities include a paddling pool for kids and a cafe.

Picture

b) You are going to London in July. Read the texts again and write notes in the table.

	Festival	Buckingham Palace	Lido
What can you see or do?			
Where is it?			
Open 25th – 29th July?			
Price for child age 14			

c) Which activity sounds the most fun? ______

0810

11 SPEAKING An argument[1] about fashion

Melanie and Joseph have different opinions[2] about fashion and clothes.

a) Complete the dialogue with words from the box.

agree • but • interested in • right • rubbish • borrow • waste of money • spend • wrong

Joseph I'm going shopping. Do you want to come?

Melanie No thanks. I'm not ____________ fashion.

Joseph Why not?

Melanie Because fashion is a ____________.

Joseph That's ________. Fashion is important! If you look good, you feel good!

Melanie I don't ________. You don't need expensive clothes to feel good!

Joseph ______ you don't have to ________ a lot of money on fashion.

Melanie You're ________. But you always spend a lot of money!

Joseph You're ________! I buy cheap clothes. But ... Melanie, can I ________ some money?

Melanie Oh!!! You're impossible[3]!

0911

3 b) Now listen and check your answers.

► SB p. 18

12 An argument about cycling

a) Complete the words in this argument.

Cycling is stupid!

R _ _ _ ish! Cycling is r _ _ lly good for you.

Maybe you're r _ _ _ t. B _ t it's dangerous.

You're w _ _ _ g! Cycling is OK if you're careful.

But c _ _ _ _ _ g is so slow!

That's t _ _ e, but it's cleaner than cars and buses.

Maybe. But I t _ _ _ k cycling is boring!

Oh, I don't a _ _ _ e! Cycling is fun!

b) Now read the argument with a partner. Read with as much feeling as you can!

► SB p. 18

[1] argument *Auseinandersetzung* [2] opinion *Meinung* [3] impossible *unmöglich*

13 LISTENING Visiting London

4 Listen to these announcements[1] in London. Tick (✓) the right answer.

1 Lies die drei möglichen Antworten, bevor du zuhörst – dann weißt du, worauf du hören sollst.
2 Viele Mitteilungen beginnen mit Floskeln wie *Ladies and gentlemen* ... oder *This is an important announcement*. Es ist also nicht schlimm, wenn du die ersten paar Wörter nicht verstehst.

1 You are in the Natural History Museum in London. Listen to the announcement. What does it tell you?
   - **a)** You have to leave the museum soon. ☐
   - **b)** The museum will open in ten minutes. ☐
   - **c)** There will be a film in ten minutes. ☐

2 You want to take the Tube. In the Tube station, you hear this announcement. What does it tell you?
   - **a)** The escalator in this Tube station isn't working. ☐
   - **b)** Please stand on the right on the escalator. ☐
   - **c)** Please stand on the left on the escalator. ☐

3 You buy your ticket and wait for the train. What does this announcement tell you?
   - **a)** Don't wait for the train on the platform. ☐
   - **b)** Don't get into the yellow train. ☐
   - **c)** Wait behind the yellow line on the platform. ☐

4 Now you're on the Tube train. Listen to the announcement. What does it tell you?
   - **a)** It tells you the name of the next station. ☐
   - **b)** The train won't stop at the next station. ☐
   - **c)** The train will stop for ten minutes at the next station. ☐

5 When you leave the train, you hear this announcement. What does it tell you?
   - **a)** Never leave your bags alone. ☐
   - **b)** You are not allowed to take big bags on the train. ☐
   - **c)** Somebody has found a bag. ☐

6 You go to a show in a London theatre. What does this announcement tell you?
   - **a)** You shouldn't take photos in the theatre. ☐
   - **b)** You should not eat or drink in the theatre. ☐
   - **c)** You should not use your mobile. ☐

1013

[1] announcement *Durchsage*

FOCUS

you can / you can't	– *du darfst / du darfst nicht; du kannst / du kannst nicht*
you should / you shouldn't	– *du solltest / du solltest nicht*
you have to / you don't have to	– *du musst / du musst nicht*

14 Safe in London

Are these sentences true or false? Write T or F.

1 When you cross the road in England you should look right, then left, then right again. ☐
2 People on escalators don't have to wait behind you if you stand on the right. ☐
3 People who can't wait can walk up or down the escalator on the right. ☐
4 When the roads are busy you should use subways. ☐
5 There can be pickpockets on buses and trains. ☐

1114

► *SB p. 20*

15 School in England and Germany

a) You're at an English school for a week. Tell the students in your class about your school in Germany. Write *have to* or *don't have to*.

1 We ______________________ stay in our classroom in breaks.

2 We ______________________ do lots of homework.

3 We ______________________ go outside in PE lessons.

b) Now write two more sentences about school with your own ideas.

1 We have to ______________________________________.

2 We don't have to ______________________________________.

c) *Max* writes an article[1] for the English school magazine. Circle the right words.

In my family in Germany we has to / have to / don't have to get up early. My dad has to / have to / doesn't have to be out of the house before 7.30 a.m., my mum earlier. But here in London my English partner has to / doesn't have to / don't have to leave the house until 8.10 a.m. I think that's great! English students have to / doesn't have to / don't have to wear a school uniform. I like that, because students doesn't have to / don't have to / have to choose what they are going to wear. Back home in Germany, my dad doesn't have to / has to / have to wear a uniform, because he's a postman, but students have to / doesn't have to / don't have to wear a uniform at school.

1115

► *SB p. 20*

[1] article *Artikel*

16 Dartford – my part of London

a) Read Natalie's text about her home town. Complete the text with words from the box.

Sometimes two verbs are possible.

can • can't • should • shouldn't • have to • don't have to

Dartford isn't a famous part of London, but it's OK. If you like shopping, you ____________ miss Bluewater. It's one of the best shopping centres in England. And if you like music, you ____________ go to a concert at the Mick Jagger Centre. Acacia Fitness is a great sports centre, but you ____________ pay and it isn't cheap.

We're near the river Thames. There's a big bridge, and cars ______ cross the bridge, but there's no cycle track so bikes ________ cross it – that's stupid! We don't have a Tube station, so if you want to go to central London you ____________ go by train.

You ________________ wait long for a train: they come very often. But there aren't any trains at night, so you ________________ leave London before 12am. *Natalie*

1216

b) Change two of Natalie's sentences for your neighbourhood.

Example: Acacia Fitness is a great sports centre, but you have to pay.
▶ The Stadtmarkt is a great market, but it isn't cheap.

1 ____.

2 ____.

▸ SB p. 21

17 Your perfect world

Imagine your perfect world. What do adults have to do? What don't young people have to do? What shouldn't teachers do? Write five ideas.

Examples: Adults have to listen to their children.
Young people don't have to get up before 10 a.m.

____

____

____

____

____

1218
1219

▸ SB p. 21

Das kann ich auf Englisch!
Hier kannst du überprüfen, ob und wie gut du alles verstanden hast. Finde auch heraus, wo du dich noch verbessern kannst. Was kannst du schon sehr gut ● oder recht gut ●? Was musst du noch üben ●? Male die Ampellichter entsprechend aus.

Unit 1

1 Ich kann etwas über London schreiben.
● Vervollständige die drei Sätze. ▶ WB S. 3, Nr. 1

1 The underground trains in London are called the ________ .

2 The ________ lives in Buckingham Palace.

3 London taxis are ________ .

2 Ich kenne viele englische Adjektive.
● Vervollständige die Sätze. ▶ WB S. 4, Nr. 3

1 My neighbourhood is ________________ , ________________ and ________________ .

2 Travelling by bus is ________________ and ________________ .

3 Travelling by plane is ________________ and ________________ .

3 Ich kann sagen, ob ich jemandem zustimme oder nicht.
● Ergänze den Dialog. ▶ WB S. 9, Nr. 11–12

I think cats are stupid.

– That's r________ ! Cats are clever – and they're fun.

– I don't ________ . They're boring and they aren't very friendly.

– You're ________ . I've got a cat and he's really friendly. He loves playing with me.

4 Ich kann sagen, was man (nicht) tun darf, kann, sollte oder muss.
● Vervollständige die Sätze mit:
can/can't should/shouldn't have to / don't have to
Bei manchen Sätzen gibt es mehr als eine Lösung. ▶ WB S. 11–12, Nr. 14–17

1 In German schools, we ________________ wear a uniform.

2 Girls ________ wear trousers at school.

3 If you want to go to the toilet, you ________________ ask the teacher .

4 You ________________ use your mobile phone in class.

1 What happened last week

Write the verbs in the simple past and (circle) the right linking words.

1 My friend Tom was ill last Tuesday and he (stay) *stayed* at home, because / so in the evening I (phone) ____________ him.

2 On Wednesday after school I (go) __________ to his house and / but we (talk) ____________ about TV programmes and (listen) _____________ to music.

3 On Thursday Tom was better so / but he (come) ___________ to school again.

4 On Friday I was ill, and I (not go) ______________ to school. I was sad and / because Tom (not phone) __________________ me.

2 TV programmes

Tom and I talked about TV. What do you think about different TV programmes? Complete the sentences.

better • funnier • sillier
more boring • more exciting •
more interesting • more popular

1 I think *soaps* are ____ than documentaries.

2 I think ____________________ are ________________________________ than reality shows.

3 I think ____________________ are ____

3 Next weekend

a) Look at the weather forecast and write what the weather will be like.

Saturday: morning	afternoon	**Sunday:** morning	afternoon

cloudy •
foggy • hot •
sunny • windy

1 On Saturday morning, it'll be __________________________________.

2 On Saturday afternoon, ______________________________________.

3 On ____.

4 ____.

b) You and Tom are going camping next weekend. Look again at the weather forecast. What will you take with you? Write five things.

We ____

____

Country life

1 A Cotswolds village

a) Write the eight words.

1 *marf* ____________
2 *upb* ____________
3 *huccrh* ____________
4 *scrasroods* ____________
5 *hpso* ____________
6 *kract* ____________
7 *dowo* ____________
8 *flide* ____________

b) Complete the sentences with the words from part a).

1 People meet, chat and drink in a ____________.
2 Animals eat grass in a ____________.
3 There are lots of trees in a ____________.
4 Two streets cross at a ____________.
5 The ____________ and the ____________ are at the crossroads.
6 There is a ____________ from the wood to the village.

1501

▸ SB p. 29

2 In town

Write the right words.

block • bus • car • fruit and veg • post • high • traffic	+	of flats • lights • office • park • street • shop • stop

1 ____________
2 ____________
3 ____________
4 ____________
5 ____________
6 ____________
7 ____________

1502

▸ SB p. 29

3 When Rob met Molly

5 a) Listen again to part of the conversation[1]. Circle the right words.

You can listen more than once.

Molly — You're new / sad here, aren't you?

Rob — Yep.

Molly — I've seen you on the train / school bus. Where are you from?

Rob — Fulham / London.

Molly — That's cool. Do you like it here in Mickleton?

Rob — No, not very much / really. There's nothing to do.

Molly — That isn't true / fair – there's lots to do. I'm Molly by the way.

Rob — Hi Molly, I'm Rob.

Molly — Well, I'll see you on the school bus on Monday / Tuesday, Rob.

Rob — Yeah, OK.

Molly got into her car / house. Rob and Wally walked quickly / home.

And Rob closed the gates carefully.

Rob — I think / Maybe Mickleton isn't so bad.

1603

b) You meet a new student at your school.
Write a conversation like a) in your exercise book.

▸ SB p. 31

4 All about *you*

a) Write the questions.

1 name What's your ? ______

2 you Where live do ? ______

3 is friend Who best your ? ______

4 are your What hobbies ? ______

b) Now write your answers.

Example: 1 My name is ...

1 ______

2 ______

3 ______

4 ______

▸ SB p. 31

[1] conversation *Gespräch*

5 Rob's family tree

Complete the sentences.

1 Denise is David and Barbara's ____________ .

2 Paul is Rob's _______ and Anna's ____________ .

3 Jodie and Evie are Rob's ________ .

4 ______________________ are Rob's parents.

5 Michael and Sarah are Evie's _________________ .

6 _______ is Rob's uncle and Anna is Rob's _______ .

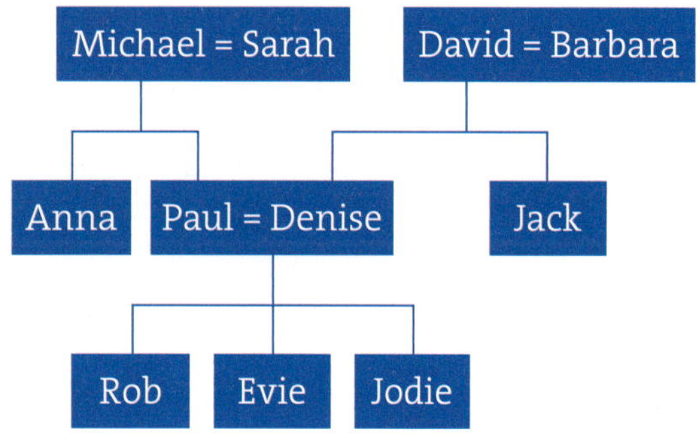

▸ SB p. 32

6 Town or country?

6

a) Rob's geography class are doing a survey[1] in town. Listen and tick (✓) the right answers.

Write notes too.

	Where do they live?		Do they like living there?		Why? Write notes.
	town	*country*	*yes*	*no*	
1	☐	☐	☐	☐	
2	☐	☐	☐	☐	
3	☐	☐	☐	☐	
4	☐	☐	☐	☐	

1706

b) What do you think about the town and the country? Write two long sentences.

The town The country	sucks	because and	you can/can't	go for walks, go shopping, go bowling, see animals, ...
	is good/ nice/boring/ OK/great		it has / it doesn't have any	cafes, parks, shops, woods ...
			it is / it isn't	quiet, noisy, safe, dangerous, ...

____

____

____

▸ SB p. 32

[1] survey *Umfrage*

7 Taking a phone message

PARTNER B: Look at page 54.

PARTNER A:

a) Copy the right sentences and complete the phone conversation.

You're welcome. Bye! | Yes, of course. I'll give him your message. | Can you spell that please?

This is Frank Berry. | Thank you. | Hello, can I talk to Mr Taylor, please? | Can I take a message?

Hello.

____

I'm sorry. He can't come to the phone right now. Who's speaking please?

____

____

Yes, it's B-E-R-R-Y.

____

Yes, can you tell him I have tickets for the cinema?

____

____

____

b) Read the conversation with your partner.

c) Now practise these phone conversations with your partner.

1 B phones. You answer the phone and start the conversation.
Write the message:

Phone messages

Message for: ______________________________

From: ______________________________

Message: ______________________________

____

Use the conversation in part a) to help you.

1807
1808

2 You phone B. B answers the phone and starts the conversation. B writes the message.
• You want to speak to Rob. Tell Partner B your name and spell it.
Your message for Rob is: the football match starts at 2pm tomorrow.

▸ SB p. 33

8 Words in the story

a) Write the words from the story.

1 Rob opened the ________ .

2 Wally put his ________ in the bushes.

3 The bags were full of ________ .

4 Suddenly they saw a ________ .

5 It had a chicken in its ________ .

6 Then they saw car ________ .

1908

b) Complete the sentences with the right time phrases.

and then • first • in the evening • later • on Saturday • suddenly • that week

1 ________ Rob and his dad put CCTV cameras in different places on the farm.

2 ________ Molly's dad still didn't feel well, so he had to stay in bed.

3 Molly and Rob watched a DVD ________ they checked the CCTV monitor.

4 ________ there was nothing, but ________ they saw a fox.

5 ________ two police officers were at the Taylors' door.

6 ________ there was an article in the Cotswolds paper.

1909

c) Write the missing words from the first part of the story.

across • along • behind • in • into • with

1 Rob and Wally ran ________ the track.

2 Molly was ________ her car.

3 Molly and Rob drove ________ the fields.

4 The sheep ran ________ the next field.

5 Molly and Missy came ________ them.

6 "You're very good ________ the sheep," Rob said.

1910

d) Check your answers in parts a, b and c on pages 34 and 35 of your book.

► SB p. 35

9 SPEAKING Describing pictures

a) You're going to talk about two pictures. Work with a partner and choose your pictures:

I'd like to talk about pictures B and D.

OK. I'll talk about A and C.

A

B

C

D

b) Make notes about your two pictures in your exercise book:

1 **Where is it?**	This is in the country / in a town / at a swimming pool	
2 **What can you see?**	I can see ... There's / there are ...	in the foreground / background in the middle / on the left /on the right
3 **What are the people doing?**	Some people are ... The dad is ...	swimming in a ... climbing a ... having a ...
4 **Something about you**	I like / don't like ... I sometimes / never go ...	

2009

c) • Now tell your partner about your pictures. Use your notes.
• Listen to your partner's talk. Does he/she talk about points 1–4?

▸ SB p. 36

10 LISTENING Talking about holiday pictures

7

a) Keira is talking about her holiday.
Look at the pictures and tick (✓) the the things you hear.

1 A

B
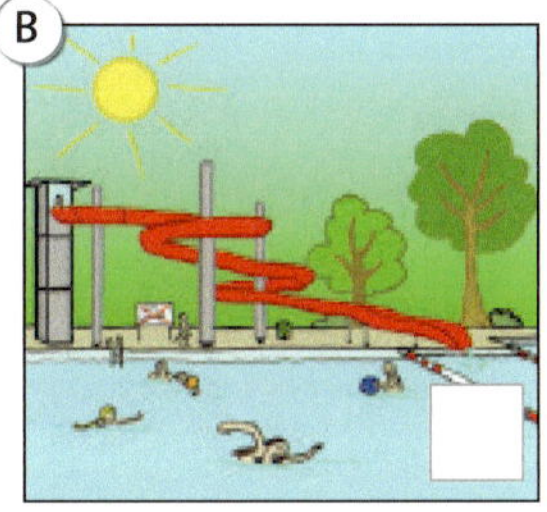
C

D

2 A

B

C

D

3 A

B

C

D

b) Listen again and tick (✓) the right option: a, b, c, or d.

1 Keira camped a) near the sea b) in a wood c) in the Cotswolds d) in Stratford-on-Avon.

2 When they put up the tent, it was a) foggy b) sunny c) snowy d) muddy.

3 The Morris dancers have a) white clothes b) no hats c) black clothes d) no shoes.

4 The first picnic was a) at the top of a hill b) in a field c) in a wood d) near cows.

5 The river was a) not too deep b) dirty c) very cold d) very dangerous.

6 The downside: a) expensive b) no beach c) unfriendly people d) nothing to do.

2110

11 WRITING Keira's holiday

a) Read Keira's text about her holiday. You are her teacher. Complete the comments[1] about her text.

My holiday in the Cotswolds

My parents, my brother and I drove to the Cotswolds.
We went to a swimming pool. We were hot.
We saw some Morris dancers.[2] They were very funny.
We had a picnic. A sheep tried to take my sandwich.
We ate in the car.
We put up our tent. It was rainy and windy. It was hard.
We went to Laverton. We had a good trip on an old train. It was expensive.
We had another picnic. It was funny. I fell into the water.

Time phrases

You should use time phrases, for example: ______ Saturday, ______ the evening, first, after ______, the next day, last weekend, then, ______ lunchtime.

Linkers

You should use linkers. Here are four examples: and, ______________________

b) Now you're Keira. Make the text better with time phrases and linkers.

My holiday in the Cotswolds

______________ my parents, my brother and I drove to the Cotswolds.

________ we went to a swimming pool __________ we were hot.

____________ we saw some Morris dancers _______ they were very funny.

________ we had a picnic. We ate in the car __________ a sheep tried to take my sandwich.

______________ we put up our tent. It was rainy and windy, _____ it was hard. ______________ we went to Laverton. We had a good trip on an old train, ________ it was expensive. ______________ we had another picnic.

It was funny __________ I fell into the water.

c) Now read what your partner wrote. Who had the better ideas?

▸ SB p. 37

2211

[1] comment *Anmerkung* [2] Morris dance *alter englischer Volkstanz*

FOCUS

the present perfect

Hiermit drückst du aus, was in der Vergangenheit (nicht) geschehen ist, wobei völlig egal ist, wann das gewesen ist. Signalwörter: ever, never, once, twice, lots of times.
Das *present perfect* besteht aus zwei Teilen:
has/have + Verb mit -ed: I have never visited London.
oder has/have + unregelmäßiges Verb: Mary has ridden a pony, but she hasn't ridden a donkey.

12 Other countries

a) Write the right verb – *has* or *have*.

Paul ___ I ______ been to Italy, but I ______ never been to Germany.

What about you, Aylin? ______ you ever been to Germany?

Aylin ___ Well, I ______ been to Turkey. And my brother ______ been to Germany. But I ______ never been to Germany.

Rob ___ I think nobody in our class ______ ever been to Germany.

Molly ___ No, you're wrong, Rob. I ______ been to Germany. It was great!

2312

b) Now find out about three students in your class. Ask about four countries and write ✔ or ✘.

	Me	Name: ______	Name: ______	Name: ______
1 Have you ever been to *Britain*?				
2 Have you ever been to ______ ?				
3 Have you ever been to ______ ?				
4 Have you ever been to ______ ?				

c) Write about what you have found out.

One student has ...
Two students have ...
No students have ...

Example: Two students have been to Britain.

1 ______

2 ______

3 ______

4 ______

► SB p. 41

13 Funny questions!

These verbs are wrong. Can you correct them?

1 "Have you ever ~~found~~ a game of cricket?" ____

2 "Have you ever ~~met~~ to Paris?" ____

3 I've never ~~ridden~~ French. Have you?" ____

4 "Have you ever ~~learned~~ a quad bike?" ____

5 "I've never ~~been~~ to a famous person. Have you?" ____

6 "I've never ~~worked~~ 20 euros in the street. Have you?" ____

2413

b) Now ask your partner the questions. Answer with **Yes, I have.** or **No, I haven't.**

▸ SB p. 41

14 Claire and her family have dreams …

What are their dreams? What haven't they done?

> I/you/we/they **haven't** …
> he/she/Dad/Mum **hasn't** …

1 I – not visit Disneyland ____

2 Mum – not open a café ____

3 My sisters – not worked in the USA ____

4 Dad – not played football for Chelsea ____

5 And we – not save any sheep! ____

▸ SB p. 41

15 Sentences about you

Write five sentences about yourself. You can use verbs in the box, or other verbs.

Example: *I've never listened to a Madonna CD. I've played tennis lots of times.*

I've	*(never)*	listened to • been to • bought • met • ridden • played • seen • talked to • had • worked • found …	*(once / twice / lots of times)*

____

____

____

____

____

2416
2417

▸ SB p. 41

Das kann ich auf Englisch!
Hier kannst du überprüfen, ob und wie gut du alles verstanden hast. Finde auch heraus, wo du dich noch verbessern kannst. Was kannst du schon sehr gut ● oder recht gut ●? Was musst du noch üben ●? Male die Ampellichter entsprechend aus.

Unit 2

1 Ich kann am Telefon etwas ausrichten.
● Vervollständige den Dialog am Telefon. ▶ WB S. 18, Nr. 7

– Hello, can I talk to Pearl please?

– I'm ________. She can't come to the phone right now. Who's ____________, please?

– This is Josh.

– Can I take a ____________, Josh?

– Can you ask her to phone me?

– Yes, of course. I'll ________ her your message.

– Thanks.

– You're ____________. Bye.

2 Ich kann sagen, wann etwas passiert.
● Wie sagt man auf Englisch: ▶ WB S. 19, Nr. 8b

1 am Samstag Vormittag ______________________________

2 letztes Wochenende ______________________

3 danach ____________________

4 am Abend ________________________

3 Ich kann ein Bild beschreiben.
● Wie kannst du sagen, wo sich etwas befindet? Ergänze vier Ausdrücke. ▶ WB S. 20, Nr. 9

In the foreground, ____

____

4 Ich kann sagen, was ich schon einmal oder noch nie getan habe.
● Ergänze die Sätze mit der richtigen Verbform.
Streiche ‚never' durch, wenn es für dich nicht stimmt. ▶ WB S. 23–24, Nr. 12–15

1 (meet) I've never ________ a famous person.

2 (visit) I've never __________ the Cotswolds.

3 (see) I've never ________ the Queen on TV.

4 (find) I've never __________ money on the street.

You know:
headache = ***Kopf****schmerzen*
football = ***Fuß****ball*

1 People

Write the words and draw arrows. The first one is done for you.

1 deha *head*

2 seno ______

3 tharto ______

4 thumo ______

5 ram ______

6 danh ______

7 elg ______

8 tofo ______

2 At the farm park

Look at the brochure. Then complete the sentences with words from the box.

can • have to – don't have to • should – shouldn't

1 Dogs ______ go into the farm park.

2 Parents ______ be with their children.

3 Are you hungry? You ______ go to *Cathy's Café*.

4 You ______ use the barbecues.

5 You can wear special clothes to the Halloween party – but you ______.

3 Plans for next weekend

What will you do next weekend?
And what won't you do?
Write some ideas.

I think I'll Perhaps I'll But I won't	go to ... • visit ... • move to ... • ride ... do ... • buy ... • listen to ... • watch ... see ... • stay in ... • drive ... • work ...

______

______

______

______

______

[1] barbecue *Grill*

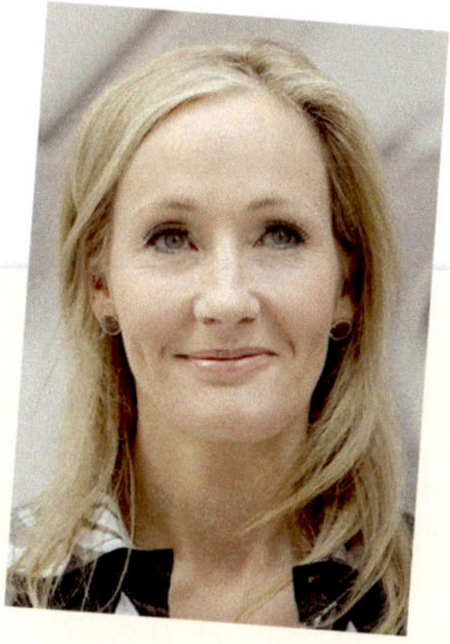

1 J. K. Rowling, the creator of Harry Potter

Read the text. Then read the sentences and tick (✓) a, b or c.

Journeys have been important in the life of Joanne Rowling, the creator of the Harry Potter books. Her mother and father first met on a train that was travelling from London to Scotland. Joanne was born in the Cotswolds, but has lived in Paris and in Portugal. But perhaps her most important journeys have been from difficult times in her life to times when her life has been much happier.

Joanne did not have a happy childhood. She didn't like her father, and her mother was often very ill. But Joanne liked writing stories when she was a child and wrote her first story when she was six. It was about a rabbit. She read her stories to her sister.

In 1990 she had the idea of writing the Harry Potter books when she was travelling on a train between Manchester and London. But she didn't have a pen, and she was too shy to ask to borrow one, so she had to remember the details in her head. She began to write her first Harry Potter book the same evening.

Later, Rowling moved to Portugal where she worked as an English teacher in the evenings. That left her free to write her book during the day. She married Jorge Arantes in 1992 and they had a daughter. But then everything went wrong.

Rowling and Arantes separated in 1993 and Rowling and her daughter moved to Scotland. She had three chapters of Harry Potter in her bag but no job, very little money, and her marriage was over. She felt really bad. But she had her daughter. And she had her big idea about Harry Potter. They gave her hope.

Rowling often went to a cafe and wrote more of her book. Her books became very popular, and Rowling is now one of the richest women in Britain. In 2001, Rowling married a second time and she and her husband Neil had a son in 2003 and a daughter in 2005. And she has given a lot of her money to organisations that help children in families in Britain and across the world.

1 Rowling's parents met
- a) in a cafe ☐
- b) in a cinema ☐
- c) on a train. ☐

2 When she was six she
- a) was ill ☐
- b) wrote her first story ☐
- c) bought a book about a rabbit. ☐

3 On the train in 1990 she
- a) thought of the Harry Potter story ☐
- b) read a story like Harry Potter ☐
- c) wrote the Harry Potter story. ☐

The words in the question are sometimes different from the words in the text – *parents / mother and father*

4 In Portugal she
- a) started her book ☐
- b) wrote more of her book ☐
- c) finished her book. ☐

5 Back in Britain, she
- a) lost all hope ☐
- b) felt much better ☐
- c) had a difficult time. ☐

6 She now has
- a) one child ☐
- b) two children ☐
- c) three children. ☐

2 Your free time

Many young people enjoy the Harry Potter books and films.

Do you like reading and watching films?
Or do you like other activities – sports, perhaps, or music?

Please write and tell us what you do in your free time.

Write a short text (60–80 words) for this teenage magazine in your exercise book. You can use some of these phrases.

after school | at the weekend | when I have time

I really don't like | waste of money

When you have finished, read what you wrote. Can you find any mistakes?

3 A trip to York

8 You want to travel to York. You fly to Manchester Airport. Now you need to take the train to York.

a) Listen to the announcements at the airport train station.

Which is your train – the first, second or third? ____________

Get ready to listen and understand. Say the times in your head before you listen.

Listen again and answer the questions.

1 When does your train leave Manchester Airport?

a) ☐ 14.41 b) ☐ 14.51 c) ☐ 15.41 d) ☐ 15.15

2 When does your train leave Manchester Piccadilly?

a) ☐ 16.11 b) ☐ 16.21 c) ☐ 17.21 d) ☐ 18.11

3 When does your train arrive in York?

a) ☐ 15.21 b) ☐ 17.36 c) ☐ 18.46 d) ☐ 19.06

b) Look at the pictures and listen to the next train announcement.
9

1 Which is the right picture: A, B or C? ☐

A

B

C

2 When will you arrive in York? ____________

Liverpool – the world in one city

1 A geography quiz

Copy the right names.

Africa • America • Australia • China • Europe • ~~India~~

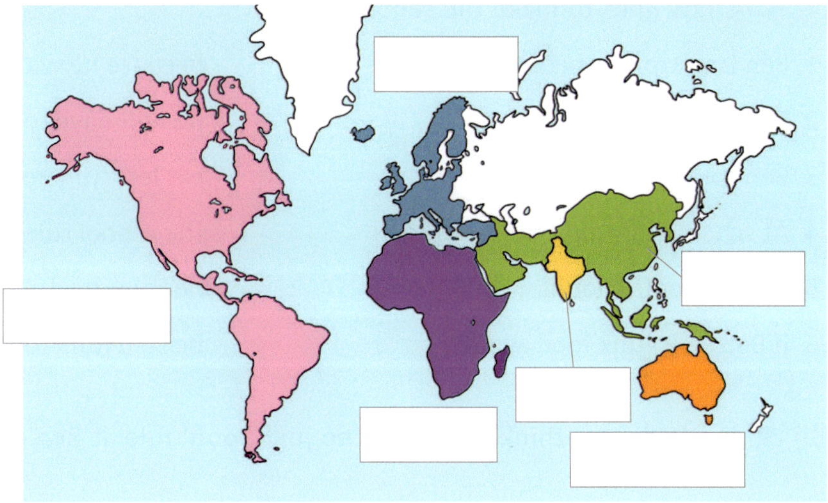

▸ SB p. 48

2 A history quiz

a) When was it? Can you guess[1]? Tick (✓) the answer you think is right.

1 The Beatles' first number 1 song	☐ 1930s	☐ 1960s	☐ 1990s
2 The first MP3 players were in the shops	☐ 1970s	☐ 1980s	☐ 1990s
3 Liverpool Football Club started	☐ 1890s	☐ 1920s	☐ 1980s
4 People could buy mobile phones for the first time	☐ 1970s	☐ 1980s	☐ 1990s
5 The start of the internet	☐ 1950s	☐ 1970s	☐ 1990s
6 The first supermarket in Britain	☐ 1930s	☐ 1950s	☐ 1970s

10 b) Listen and check your answers. How many did you get right?

▸ SB p. 49

3 A profile of Liverpool

Complete the table with the words in the box.

Liverpool One • museums • Liverpool and Everton • important harbour • England • ferry trip • shopping • The Beatles • slaves

LIVERPOOL			
Where		Famous people from Liverpool	
Things to do or see		History	
Shopping centre		Football clubs	

▸ SB p. 49

[1] guess *raten*

4 Ben's problem at school

a) Draw lines to make the sentences.

1 Ben is in trouble because ...	because he wanted to make some money.
2 That was against ...	he will have to go home for a week.
3 Ben sold food ...	eat less junk food.
4 At school, they only sell ...	the school rules.
5 The students should ...	healthy food.
6 If Ben sells junk food again ...	he sold junk food at school.

3004

b) What do you think about the 'no junk food' rule at Ben's school? Write a sentence.

___

► SB p. 51

5 Healthy or junk?

a) What do you think about these things to eat and drink? Write them in group A, B, or C.

biscuits • soup • hot dogs • salad • chips • cereal bars • brown bread • chocolate bars • vegetables • energy drinks • fruit juice • crisps • fish • sweets • apples
… and four more things to eat/drink

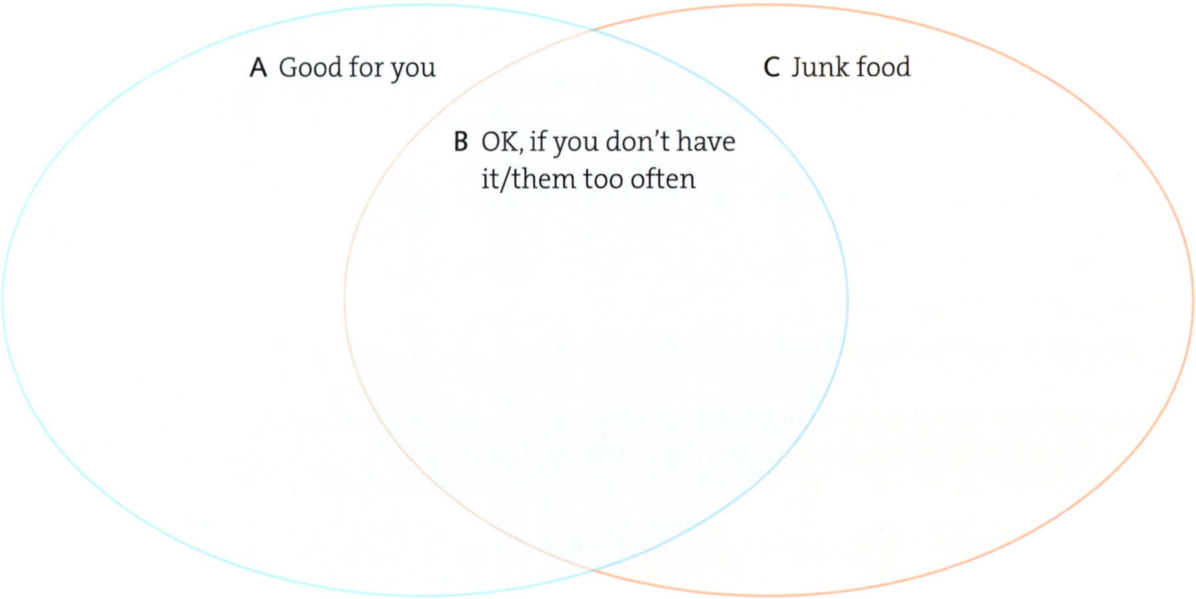

c) Now find out if your partner thinks the same as you.

I think biscuits are junk food. What do you think?

I think they're OK if you don't have them too often.

► SB p. 51

6 What are they thinking?

Read each sentence and draw a line to the person who thinks it.

The sentences aren't the same as in your book.

Mrs Fox

1 Why aren't you as active in class as you were last term?

2 I can't do school work well.

3 You're joking!

4 Aren't you the best salesperson in the school?

5 You could take part in this competition.

6 I don't want to get into trouble.

7 Maybe ... I'm not sure.

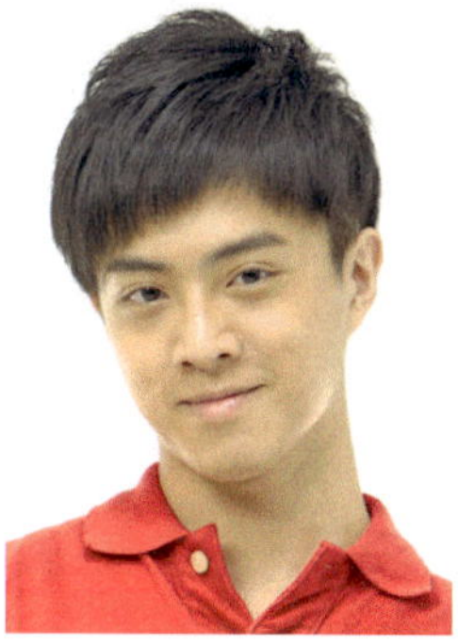

Ben

▸ SB p. 52

7 Talking about business

11

Listen to one team talking about the competition. Answer the questions.

Listen to part 1 and answer question 1. Then do part 2, ... etc

1 a) Look at the pictures A–F. Tick (✓) the things the students talk about.

A  T-shirts

B  Cereal bars

C  Sandwiches

D 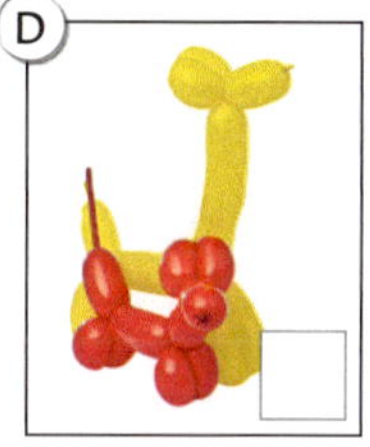 Animal ballons

E  Plants

F  Hot dogs

b) What will they sell? A ☐ B ☐ C ☐ D ☐ E ☐ F ☐

2 When will they sell them?

a) ☐ after school b) ☐ at lunchtime c) ☐ at break

3 *Two days later ...*

a) What price can they sell them for?

a) ☐ 40p b) ☐ 50p c) ☐ 60p

b) What profit could they make?

a) ☐ £35 b) ☐ £40 c) ☐ £45

4 a) What name do they give the business?

a) ☐ Barz 4 Kidz b) ☐ Food 4 Kidz c) ☐ Healthy Bars

b) What do <u>you</u> think of their business name? (cool? stupid? funny? clever?)

3107

I think it's ______________________________

▸ SB p. 53

8 Mr Chung helps Ben

a) What does Ben's dad say? Find the words in the puzzle (→ ↓) and write the missing letters.

Son, to do well in B _ _ _ _ _ _ S you have to work H _ _ D and S _ _ L lots of cakes. Your cupcakes must be something S _ _ _ _ _ L. You need to make a P _ _ _ _ T, of course, and be a good S _ _ _ _ _ _ _ _ _ N, but it also helps if you're L _ _ _ Y!

B	U	S	I	N	E	S	S
E	M	A	E	G	J	R	E
J	D	L	D	B	E	F	L
S	P	E	C	I	A	L	L
A	E	S	N	L	F	U	D
F	M	P	X	D	A	C	S
C	S	E	V	G	X	K	Y
H	A	R	D	K	G	Y	U
F	T	S	M	B	O	R	L
P	R	O	F	I	T	D	F
I	O	N	Y	R	W	A	B

b) How does Ben's story end?
Two words in these sentences are wrong. Find them and write the correct sentences.

Ben's team made healthy 'Beatles' scones. They didn't win, but they were third.

____

____

▸ SB p. 55

9 Ben's friend Grace is in the competition too

Read what Grace says and write the missing words in the story.

amazing • broken • enough • flour • good at • impressed • mean • negative • on TV • take part

I wanted to __________ in the competition, so I made some scones. The kitchen was really messy and there was ________ and ________ egg everywhere. Then mum came home. She was really angry! An hour later, I gave mum a scone. She wasn't __________. "It's OK, but it's not good ________ for a competition," she said. "What do you ________, Mum?" I asked. "Well, everyone can make scones," she said. I felt really fed up. An hour later, mum came back into the kitchen. "Sorry I was so __________," she said. "You're __________ making scones, Grace. Why don't you make scones that are really different?" "Like ... hm ... *banana* scones?" "That's a great idea!" she said. "Banana scones will be __________!" So now I'm making banana scones. If I win, I'll be ________!

3209

▸ SB p. 55

10 READING & NOTE-TAKING **Who is Louis Smith?**

a) You're going to find out about Louis Smith.
First read these notes. This is the information you want:

Louis Smith

What his sport is: ____________________

Where he's from: ____________________

What he did when he was 19: ____________________

Why 2012 was a special year – what he did in the summer: ____________________

What he did after that: ____________________

3310

b) • Read the article. Underline in the article the information you need for the notes.
• Now write the information in the notes.

Louis Smith – what a star!

gold silver bronze

2012 was very special for Louis Smith. He was the star of the British gymnastics team – and he was on a TV reality show too!

Louis is from the south-east of England. His mother is English; his father is from Jamaica. In 2008, when Louis was only 19, he won a bronze medal in the Olympics.

In 2012, he wanted to win the gold medal! But World Champion Krisztian Berki wanted it too. The competition was very exciting. Louis got 9.066 points – but Berki got 9.166! Berki won gold by only 0.1 point! But Louis was still happy – he won a silver medal.

After the Olympics, Louis took part in a popular reality TV show: a dancing competition. At first, people weren't impressed. They said Louis wasn't good at dancing. But he worked hard with his competition partner, Flavia, and every week they got better and better!

But could they win the competition? In the last week, their dance was amazing! Who won the TV dancing competition? Louis and Flavia! Louis was so happy: "Now I've won something in 2012!" he said.

c) SPEAKING
• Use the notes. Practise a short talk about Louis Smith.
• Give the talk to your partner. *"Today, I'm going to talk about ... His sport is ..."*

► SB p. 56

11 Is there too much football on TV?

a) READING Lily says …

I think there's too much football on TV!

Do Lily's friends agree or disagree with her? Read what they say. Write agree or disagree.

I ______________. There are lots of other exciting sports too.

I ______________. I think football is very popular.

I ______________. Families can watch football together on TV – that's nice.

I ______________ with Lily. People sit and watch TV. They should do a sport!

I ______________. Football on TV is good, because tickets for matches are expensive.

I ______________ with Lily. Football is brilliant, and the matches are really exciting!

I ______________. The players are sometimes a bit violent and the fans often fight.

I ______________ with Lily. Footballers aren't always good role models.

b) LISTENING Listen to four people talking and circle the right words. 12

Amy ___ Do you think there's too much football on TV?

Joe ___ No, I don't. It's true – there *is* a lot of football on TV, but not too much. Everybody / nobody likes football.

Ali ___ That's rubbish! Lots of people think football is amazing / boring. What do you think, Amy?

Amy ___ Well, in my opinion, football matches are a waste of time / money.

Kayla ___ I agree. There are lots of other exciting sports. For example, I'd like to watch more skiing / boxing on TV.

Ali ___ You're joking! That's too violent / boring.

Kayla ___ That's rubbish! And I think that some football players are violent – they aren't good role models / sportsmen.

Ali ___ Maybe you're right.

Joe ___ I disagree. I think footballers work hard / a lot. They do lots of training. And secondly, I think football is great because everyone can play. Kids / boys watch it on TV, then they go out and play football in the street. It makes them healthy / fit!

3411

c) Look at parts a) and b) again. Highlight opinions that you agree with.

d) WRITING What do you think?

- Lily says, "I think there's too much football on TV!" Do you agree or disagree with Lily?

____

- Write three sentences about why you agree or disagree.

In my opinion ... I think ...

You can use ideas from a) and b)!

____

____

____

____

____

e) WRITING Complete these 'opinion' phrases.

disagree • I • opinion • right • rubbish • you're

1 In my ____________ ...
2 Maybe you're ____________ .
3 That's ____________ .
4 ____________ wrong!
5 I ____________ .
6 ____________ agree.

f) SPEAKING Is there too much football on TV?

- Discuss[1] this in groups of three or four.

Use ideas from d) and phrases from e).

- How many people in your group think ...

there is too much football on TV? ______ / there isn't too much football on TV? ______

[1] discuss *besprechen*

► SB p. 57

12 MEDIATION Things to do in Liverpool

Your uncle is going to Liverpool. Your English friend sends you some ideas about things he can do there. Answer your uncle's questions in German.

Weißt du noch? Du brauchst nicht jedes Wort zu übersetzen.

A

I've been to the Maritime Museum, and it's really good. It's all about Liverpool and the sea.

The museum has lots of different parts – for example you can learn about Liverpool and smuggling[1], slaves, the Titanic – and lots more. I think your uncle would like it.

Maritime Museum
Free entry!
open every day 10 am–5 pm

1 Worum geht's im Museum? __________

2 Was zahlen Erwachsene und Kinder? __________

3 Worum geht es in den verschiedenen Abteilungen? __________

B

Another idea for your uncle is a tour of the Beatles' houses – where John Lennon and Paul McCartney lived when they were children! You go by minibus.

If your uncle is a Beatles fan, he'll love this! You can go inside the houses and see their bedrooms, living rooms, etc. It sounds amazing!

THE BEATLES
CHILDHOOD HOMES TOURS
March – October:
Tours leave from the city centre at 10 am, 11 am and 2.15 pm.
Prices: adult £20, child: £5

4 Was für eine Tour ist es? __________

5 Was zahlen Erwachsene und Kinder? __________

6 Sieht man die Häuser bloß von außen? __________

7 Findet die Tour im August statt? __________

▸ SB p. 58

3612

[1] smuggling *Schmuggel*

FOCUS

If + simple present + future will/'ll *or* won't	If	I win	I'll be very happy.
	If	Ben wins	he will go to London.
	If	he loses	he won't be too sad.

13 Biz 4 Kidz – the teacher

Mrs Fox is thinking about Ben and the competition.
Circle the right form of the simple present.

If Ben take / takes part in the competition, his team will make a profit.

If Ben start / starts to be more active in class, he'll be happier.

If our students win / wins the competition, they'll go to London.

But if they lose / loses, I won't be too disappointed.

If Ben do / does well, his dad will be impressed.

3713

▸ SB p. 61

14 Biz 4 Kidz – Team 1 "Food 4 U"

Team 1 are talking about what to make.
Put the right words in the sentences.

1 If we make cupcakes, everybody ______________ them. — will want / will go

2 If it's hot, customers ______________ soup. — won't read / won't buy

3 If it's cold, nobody ______________ ice cream. — will take part in / will eat

4 If we make cakes, my mum ______________ us. — will mean / will help

5 If the price is 60p per cake, ______________ a good profit. — we'll make / we'll think

6 If we win ______________ on TV! — we'll be / we'll see

3714

▸ SB p. 61

15 Biz 4 Kidz – Team 2 "Balloons R Us"

Anushka is in the "Balloons R Us" team with Gemma.
Write the missing words.

won't go • 'll read • will buy • 'll be • won't be • 'll make

If we take part in the Biz 4 Kidz competition, it ______________ fun – so if we don't win,

I ______________ too sad. My business partner Gemma ______________ lots of balloons

at the supermarket. I ______________ the book about making things with balloons,

so I ______________ with her. Then on Sunday we ______________ our balloon animals.

3715

▸ SB p. 61

16 Biz 4 Kidz – Team 3 "Gold!"

Write these words in the right order.

1 If / to the hospital / a profit / we make / we'll give it

If we make ____________________

2 If / too sad / we won't be / we lose

If ____________________

3 If / we'll be / we win / happy / very

If ____________________

4 If / will be impressed / we're / my friends / on TV

If ____________________

3816

► SB p. 61

17 What will next weekend be like?

a) Write the verb in the simple present.

b) Finish the sentence with words from the box ("I'll be …").

I'll be … • happy • fed up • tired • excited • disappointed • sad • angry • amazed • glad

1 If it ________ *(rain)*, *I'll be* ____________________

2 If my teacher ________ *(give)* me lots of homework, *I'll* ____________________

3 If my friends ________ *(come)* to my house, ____________________

4 If I ________ *(have)* to go to the supermarket, ____________________

5 If a dog ________ *(eat)* my mobile, ____________________

► SB p. 61

18 In the next holidays

Write the verbs in the right forms.

If we ________ *(have)* enough money, we ________ *(go)* to Britain on holiday this year. We'd like to stay for three weeks, but if my dad ______ *(be)* busy at work, we ________ *(stay)* for two weeks. If my older brother ______ *(have)* time, he ________ *(come)* with us. If he ________ *(come)*, he ________ *(bring)* his girlfriend too. If she ________ *(want)* to come, I ________ *(be)* glad, because she speaks English very well. If I ______ *(try)* to speak English on holiday, she ________ *(help)* me.

3818
3819
3820

► SB p. 61

Das kann ich auf Englisch!
Hier kannst du überprüfen, ob und wie gut du alles verstanden hast. Finde auch heraus, wo du dich noch verbessern kannst. Was kannst du schon sehr gut ● oder recht gut ●? Was musst du noch üben ●? Male die Ampellichter entsprechend aus.

Unit 3

1 Ich kenne den Wortschatz für Essen und Getränke.
● Nenne fünf gesunde Lebensmittel und fünf Lebensmittel, die nicht so gesund sind .

▶ WB S. 30, Nr. 5

Gesund: fruit juice, ______________________________

Nicht so gesund: ______________________________

2 Ich kann über Geschäftliches sprechen.
● Was bedeuten diese Ausdrücke auf Deutsch?

▶ WB S. 32, Nr. 8

1 You have to work hard.

____

2 Your cupcakes must be something special.

____

3 You need to make a good profit.

____

3 Ich kann meine Meinung sagen.
● Schreibe das Gegenteil:

▶ WB S. 34–35, Nr. 11

1 Sport is interesting! Sport is __________ !

2 I agree. I __________ .

3 You're wrong! You're __________ !

4 I don't like it. I __________ it.

4 Ich kann sagen, was passieren wird, wenn ...
● Schreibe was du dieses Wochenende machen wirst, wenn es sonnig ist *(3 Ideen)* und wenn es regnet *(3 Ideen)*.

▶ WB S. 37–38, Nr. 13–18

If it's sunny, I'll go cycling, or I'll ______________________________

____

If it rains, ______________________________

____

REVISION

1 Transport words

Match the transport to the place you can find it. Draw lines.

1 plane	bus stop
2 ferry	harbour
3 bus	garage
4 Tube train	airport
5 car	station

2 Places in the High Street

Read the sentences and write the numbers on the map.

The ① pub is at the crossroads, next to the tree.
There's a ② letter box under the tree.
The ③ post office is between the pub and the track.
The ④ hairdresser is at the crossroads, on the left, next to the church.
Next to the post office, on the right of the track, is a ⑤ block of flats.
The post office has a small ⑥ field behind it, next to the track.
In front of the block of flats there's a ⑦ bus stop.
There are three ⑧ cows in the middle of the field.

Scotland is different

1 Things to see in Scotland

Copy the right titles for the pictures.

Edinburgh Castle • mountains • Loch Ness • modern buildings • Scottish dancing • the Scottish flag

1 

2 

3 

4 

5 

6 

4101

▸ SB p. 69

2 A Scottish puzzle

a) Write the words in the puzzle. All the words are on pages 68 and 69 of your book.

1 a terrible big animal
2 It's Berlin in Germany and Paris in France.
3 lots and lots of trees together
4 what people wear
5 schools, hospitals, train stations, banks, etc
6 what Scottish people call a 'loch'
7 what people speak
8 the capital of Scotland

1			S							
			2 C							
	3		O							
4			T							
5			L							
		6	A							
	7		N							
		8	D							

4102

b) The yellow letters make the name of the city of ____________ .

▸ SB p. 69

3 News for the MacDonalds

13

a) Listen to the MacDonalds again. Tick (✓) the right answer.

1 Alec MacDonald has just a) ☐ got up b) ☐ phoned a friend c) ☐ come home.

2 His bad news is that the shop
a) ☐ is very cold b) ☐ will maybe close c) ☐ is under water.

3 Kate MacDonald lost her job a) ☐ a year ago b) ☐ last week c) ☐ last month.

4 Alec and Kate talk to their children in
a) ☐ the kitchen b) ☐ Jamie's room c) ☐ the living room.

5 Alec MacDonald will maybe have to work in
a) ☐ Glasgow b) ☐ Edinburgh c) ☐ Inverness.

6 That's a long way by train from where they live:
a) ☐ 70 miles away b) ☐ 117 miles away c) ☐ 170 miles away

b) Tick (✓) the right ending.

The children are sad because ...

a) ... they want to watch a good film on TV, but their parents want to talk. ☐

b) ... their dad's shop will maybe close, and he'll maybe have to live far away. ☐ 4203

c) ... a shop in town is going to close. Jamie buys clothes there, and Kara works there at weekends. ☐

► SB p. 70

4 Who thought this?

a) Read the MacDonalds' discussion on page 71 of your book again. Then match the people with the thought bubbles[1] (1–8). Draw lines.

1 I've lost my job and now the family has a problem.

2 Dad shouldn't blame himself.

3 The family should all be in one place when there is a problem.

4 I know the answer to our problem!

Mr McDonald

Mrs McDonald

Kara

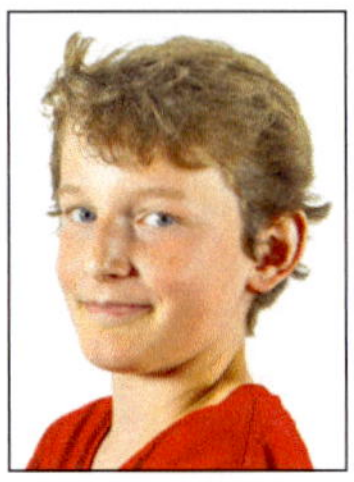
Jamie

5 We'll open our house as a Bed & Breakfast.

6 I'm not sure about the B&B idea.

7 It's a good idea. We can teach ourselves how to make money as a B&B.

8 We don't have to say 'yes' or 'no' today. 4204

► SB p. 71

[1] thought bubble *Gedankenblase*

5 The family are talking about the problem

Complete the sentences with the words in blue from the box.

I you he she we you they	blame enjoy help look after teach	myself yourself himself herself ourselves yourselves themselves

Mum — Dad blames __________ for this problem.

Kara — That's silly, Dad! My friend's mum taught __________ how to make money from a B&B, and you can teach __________ too.

Dad — If we open a B&B, we won't have much time for you kids.

Kara — Don't worry, we can look after __________ !

Jamie — I can help __________ to toast in the morning. You won't have to make breakfast for me!

Kara — If you start a B&B, I think you and Mum will enjoy __________ !

Mum — And we live in a great place – the people who stay here will enjoy __________ too!

4305

▸ SB p. 71

6 MEDIATION A Highland B&B

Your dad wants to have a holiday in Scotland. Read this advert for a B&B and answer his questions in German.

Don't worry – you don't have to understand every word!

Bonniebank Bed and Breakfast

We are a friendly Bed and Breakfast on the banks of Loch Alsh in the beautiful Scottish Highlands.

Accommodation: We have a twin room and a family room (sleeps 5). Both rooms have TV, radio, wifi internet, plus hairdryer and tea and coffee facilities.

The area is ideal for outdoor activities: walking, mountain climbing, fishing, etc. You can borrow fishing equipment from us. We are also near Eilean Donan Castle.

Open: April to November   Price: £28 per person per night

Vegetarian options • Dogs welcome

1 Wir sind zu fünft – gibt es ein Zimmer in dieser Größe? __________

2 Was kostet es? __________

3 Gibt es DVD-Player auf dem Zimmer? __________

4 Was kann man in der Umgebung unternehmen?

____

5 Muss man einen Fön mitbringen? __________

▸ SB p. 72

7 Making a reservation

a) Put the dialogue into the right order. Write the missing numbers.

☐	Do you need directions, Mrs Craig?
☐	A reservation? Of course. Which room do you want?
☐	That's great, Mrs Craig. See you in May, then. Bye.
1	Hello, this is Bonniebank Bed and Breakfast.
☐	The twin room, please.
7	Yes, the room is free then. What's your name please?
☐	It's Mrs Craig. C-R-A-I-G.
☐	The twin room, OK ... And for what dates?
☐	No, we'll be OK, thanks. We have a GPS.
12	Thank you. Goodbye.
☐	Friday the 5th of May, for three nights.
☐	Hello. I'd like to make a reservation, please.

▸ SB p. 73

4407

14 b) Now listen and check your answer.

8 Phone messages

15 Four guests phone Bonniebank B&B. Listen to the phone calls and write the information.

1 **Telephone reservations**

Room	family
Date of arrival[1]	11
How many nights	
Guest's name	Mr

2 **Telephone reservations**

Room	
Date of arrival	17 August
How many nights	
Guest's name	Mrs Hirst

3 **Telephone reservations**

Room	
Date of arrival	21 July
How many nights	
Guest's name	Pirie

4 **Telephone reservations**

Room	twin
Date of arrival	
How many nights	1
Guest's name	

4408

▸ SB p. 73

[1] Arrival *Ankunft*

9 Telephone reservations

PARTNER B: Look at page 55.

PARTNER A:
Practise these phone conversations with your partner.

1 Answer the phone and start the conversation. The notes will help you. Write the message.

- *Hello, Bonniebank Bed & Breakfast*
- *which room?*
- *for what dates?*
- *yes, room is free – name?*
- *great – see you then – bye*

Telephone reservations	
Room	______
Date of arrival	______
How many nights	______
Guest's name	______

2 Phone partner B. He/She starts the conversation. The notes will help you.

- *make a reservation*
- *family*
- *16th July, 3 nights*
- (say your name, and spell it)
- *bye*

▸ SB p. 73

10 PEOPLE AND PLACES Welcome to Scotland

a) Watch the DVD again and put the four pictures in the order you saw them. Write 1, 2, 3, 4 in the boxes. Then underline the right word in each sentence.

b) Now watch again and check your answers.

▸ SB p. 73

11 What happened in the story?

a) Answer the questions for the parts of the story that you read.

Part A Write the right verbs in the sentences.

answered • came • chatted • enjoyed • found • heard • said • took

1 The Grants ________ into the house and the old man ________ them upstairs.

2 "Maybe there are ghosts," Abi ________ and laughed. "Ghosts don't exist," mum ________.

3 Later the Grants ________ and ________ the food.

4 The next morning the Grants ________ the place empty and they ________ lonely music.

Part B Circle the right answers.

1 When the Grants landed at the airport, they couldn't find one of their bags / children.

2 Then Mrs Grant said that her money / driving licence was missing.

3 They hired a car, and at first, Mr Grant drove on the right / left – the wrong side[1] in Britain!

4 When they saw a sign to Loch Ness, Mr Grant thought, "Things are looking bad / better."

Part C Answer these questions. Write sentences.

1 Where did the Grants arrive first? *They arrived* ________

2 What did they tell the McDonalds? *They told them about* ________

____

3 Why were the Grants excited about Urquhart castle? *They were excited because* ________

____

4 What was Urquhart castle like? *It was* ________

____

Part D Find the reasons and write the right letters.

1 It was difficult to drive at first ...	☐	a **because** their mobiles didn't work in the mountains.
2 They knew they weren't in Dores ...	☐	b **because** they told him about their problems.
3 They couldn't phone ...	☐	c **because** they could only see woods and fields.
4 They noticed the building ...	☐	d **because** they saw a light.
5 The man invited them to stay ...	☐	e **because** it was dark and the road was narrow.

4611

16 b) Now listen to the story again and check your answers.

► SB p. 75

[1] side *Straßenseite*

12 WRITING When a different person tells the story …

Duncan is writing about what happened in Scotland.
Read his text and write the missing words.

dad • I • mum • we

In dieser Aufgabe handelt es sich um 'Perspektiv-Wechsel'. Das heißt, du erzählst die Geschichte aus der Sicht einer anderen Person. Also: 'the Grant family' / 'they' ► 'we' 'Duncan' ► 'I' usw

~~The Grant family~~ *We* came into the big old house. ~~They~~ ______ went with the old man to a room with four beds. ~~Duncan and Abi~~ ______ were very excited. "This is a real Scottish castle," ~~Duncan~~ ______ said. "Maybe there are ghosts!" Abi said and laughed. "Ghosts don't exist," ~~Mrs Grant~~ ______ answered. Later in the evening ~~the family~~ ______ went down to a big kitchen. ~~The Grants~~ ______ chatted, enjoyed the food and danced. "Our family left Scotland more than 200 years ago," ~~Mr Grant~~ ______ said. "Then you're welcome home," the old man said. But the next morning, ~~the Grants~~ ______ found the place empty. ~~They~~ ______ saw the old man on the walls of the castle. ~~The Grants~~ ______ waved but the old man just played his bagpipes.

4712

► SB p. 76

13 WRITING Your amazing day

T = Write a time phrase (your own ideas).
L = Write a linker (so, but, and, because).

We left our house **T** *at six o'clock in the morning*. I slept in the car **L** *because* I was very tired. We arrived at the theme park **T** ______________ . I went on the big wheel[1]. It was great **L** ______ it was a bit scary too. I wanted something scarier **L** ______ I went on the rollercoaster[2]. That was really scary **L** ________ it was so fast. We all had lunch together **T** ______________ . **T** ______________ my brother and I went on the bumper cars[3]. It was an amazing day **L** ______ we were very happy when we drove home.

4713

► SB p. 76

[1] big wheel *Riesenrad* [2] rollercoaster *Achterbahn* [3] bumper car *Autoscooter*

14 READING The Wild Highlands

a) Skim this text to find out what it is about. Tick (✓) the right answer.

Remember – when you skim a text, you don't need to read and understand every word.

The text is:

a) ☐ a story about castles in the Highlands

b) ☐ a tourist brochure about the Highlands

c) ☐ an article about people who have been to the Highlands

d) ☐ an article about making films in the Highlands.

The Wild Highlands of Scotland

It's funny ... You've never been to Scotland, but when you look at photos of the Highlands, in a book or on the internet, you think that you've seen the Highlands before. Why is that? I'll tell you why: you've seen this beautiful countryside at the cinema!

Film directors from Hollywood to Bollywood like to make films in Scotland, because the mountains and lakes in the Scottish Highlands are so beautiful. In many places, there's no traffic, no noise of traffic – and no people! These lonely, wild, beautiful places are ideal for filming.

Lots of famous films have scenes filmed in the Highlands – the Harry Potter films; "Skyfall", the James Bond film; the Batman film "The Dark Knight Rises"; Ridley Scott's science fiction film "Prometheus" and many more. The Hogwarts express train to Harry Potter's school is a real steam train in the west of Scotland. It travels from Mallaig to Fort William in summer. You can travel on it yourself!

b) Look at the article again. Are these sentences *True* or *False*?

	True	False
1 Hollywood directors[1] make films in the Highlands because it's cheap.	☐	☐
2 There are no mountains in the Highlands.	☐	☐
3 Many parts of the Highlands are very quiet.	☐	☐
4 You can see the Highlands in many famous films.	☐	☐
5 The James Bond film "Skyfall" has scenes filmed[2] in Scotland.	☐	☐
6 You can go on the 'Hogwarts' train at Christmas.	☐	☐

c) Have you seen any of the films in the article?

► SB p. 78

1 director *Regisseur* 2 film (verb) *drehen*

FOCUS

the people who ..., the things that ...

Use **who** and **that** when you describe people and things.
- Use **who** with people: That's the man who played the bagpipes at the festival!
- Use **that** with things: Where's the map that we bought in Edinburgh?

15 A puzzle

a) Find the correct words for 1–5.

1 the beautiful place in Scotland that has mountains
2 an animal that you can ride
3 a person who drives
4 people who visit you at your house
5 a person who helps you with your car

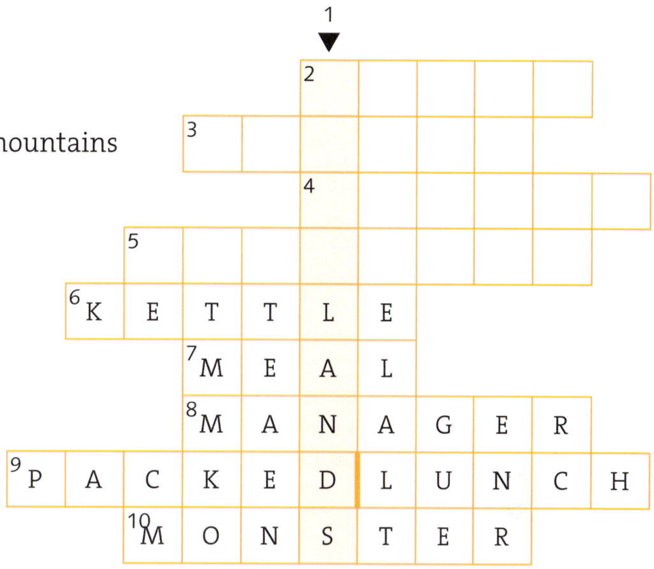

4915

b) Write clues for 6–10. You can use these words to make your clues:

food the person an animal something	that who	you eat in the morning, afternoon and evening is boss in a shop or hotel is big and terrible you use to make hot water for tea. you take with you to eat in the middle of the day

6 ______

7 ______

8 ______

9 ______

10 ______

4916

c) Guess the words.

PARTNER B: Go to page 55

PARTNER A: Write clues for these words in your exercise book.
Can your partner guess the words?

cafe breakfast champion

► SB p. 81

16 GAME How do you say it?

17 **a)** Look at the pictures in the snake. Listen. What things does the girl need? Write the numbers.

17, ________________

b) With a partner, describe[1] three things in the game. Here are some ideas:

I need a thing that you use to ... I need some stuff that you use to ...

- wash / dry yourself
- make fire
- carry things
- make the room dark
- cook / cut food
- look at yourself
- ...

c) Play this game in groups of three or four students. You need a dice and counters. When you land on a picture, describe what you need. If you can't, go back two places.

[1] describe *beschreiben*

5017
5018

► SB p. 81
► Wordbank p. 63

PORTFOLIO

Das kann ich auf Englisch!
Hier kannst du überprüfen, ob und wie gut du alles verstanden hast. Finde auch heraus, wo du dich noch verbessern kannst. Was kannst du schon sehr gut ● oder recht gut ●? Was musst du noch üben ●? Male die Ampellichter entsprechend aus.

Unit 4

1 Ich kann ein Gespräch in einer Pension oder einem Hotel führen.
● Was bedeuten diese Ausdrücke auf Deutsch? ▶ WB S. 43, Nr. 6

1 We have a twin room ...

____

2 ... and a family room for five people.

____

3 It costs £28 per person per night.

____

4 The rooms have a TV and Wi-fi.

____

2 Ich kann ein Zimmer buchen.
● Ergänze diese Email. ▶ WB S. 44, Nr. 7

Subject: Reservation

Dear Mr Martin

We'd like to make a __________ please. We'd like to book your twin __________

for three __________ from Friday, 19th July. Will the room be __________ ?

Thank you very much.

S Formby and G Spencer

3 Ich kann nach Sachen fragen, auch wenn ich das eigentliche Wort nicht kenne.
● Ergänze diese Sätze mit who oder that.
Und weißt du das Wort? Trage es ein. ▶ WB S. 49–51, Nr. 15–16

1 I need the thing ______ you use to dry yourself after a shower. (a __________)

2 What do you call the person ______ brings you food in a restaurant? (a __________)

3 Where's the thing ______ you use to make hot water for tea? (the __________)

4 I want to speak to the person ______ is the boss in this hotel. (the __________)

1 Food on a Scottish holiday

a) You're in a Scottish B&B and your mum is looking at the breakfast menu. Read the menu and your mum's questions.

Why not try our homemade porridge for a really healthy start to the day?
Or enjoy our cooked Scottish breakfast with:
bacon, egg, potato scones, black pudding, kippers, tomatoes and mushrooms
... and toast or oatcakes
You can drink tea or coffee (with milk or cream) and orange juice.

1 Porridge ist Haferbrei. Frage mal, ob sie den mit Milch und Zucker machen.

2 *Potato scones* – sind das die kleinen Kuchen, die man mit Marmelade und Sahne isst?

3 Frag doch mal, was *black pudding* ist. Und was sind *kippers*?

b) How can you ask your mum's questions in English?

1 Do you make porridge ______

2 Are they the scones that ______

3 What is ______

18 **c)** Listen and check.

19 **d)** Now listen to the waiter and answer your mum's questions in German.

– Der Haferbrei wird mit ______

– Potato scones isst man mit ______

– Black pudding ist ______ und Kipper ist Fisch.

2 Our hiking trip

Write the verbs in the simple past.

Mum and I *(have)* had three days in the Highlands. On the first day we *(go)* ______ hiking in the mountains. It was cold, so we *(wear)* ______ warm clothes. We *(pack)* ______ lots of food and *(take)* ______ a good map. We *(want)* ______ to climb Ben Nevis, Scotland's highest mountain. It's only 1344 metres high, but we *(not get)* ______ to the top, because it *(start)* ______ to snow! I *(not know)* ______ the weather was like that in Scotland. We *(come)* ______ back down the mountain and *(eat)* ______ our food in the car.

7 Taking a phone message

PARTNER B

a) Copy the right sentences and complete the phone conversation.

You're welcome. Bye! | Yes, of course. I'll give him your message. | Can you spell that please?

This is Frank Berry. | Thank you. | Hello, can I talk to Mr Taylor, please? | Can I take a message?

Hello.

______

I'm sorry. He can't come to the phone right now. Who's speaking please?

______

______

Yes, it's B-E-R-R-Y.

______

Yes, can you tell him I have tickets for the cinema?

______

______

______

b) Read the conversation with your partner.

Use the conversation in part a) to help you.

c) Now practise these phone conversations with your partner.

1 You phone A. A answers the phone and starts the conversation. A writes the message.
- You want to speak to Molly. Tell A your name and spell it.
  Your message for Molly is: there's a really good concert on Saturday night.

2 A phones. You answer the phone and start the conversation. Write the message:

Phone messages

Message for: ______

From: ______

Message: ______

______

▸ WB p. 18

9 Telephone reservations

PARTNER B

Practise these phone conversations with your partner.

1 Phone partner A. He/She starts the conversation.
The notes will help you.

- *make a reservation*
- *twin*
- *10th July, 5 nights*
- (say your name, and spell it)
- *bye*

2 Answer the phone and start the conversation.
The notes will help you.
Write the message.

- *Hello, Bonniebank Bed & Breakfast*
- *which room?*
- *for what dates?*
- *yes, room is free – name?*
- *great – see you then – bye*

Telephone reservations

Room	______
Date of arrival	______
How many nights	______
Guest's name	______

▸ *WB p. 45*

15 A puzzle

c) Guess the words.

Write clues for these words in your exercise book.
Can your partner guess the words?

sleeping bag **neighbour** **dinosaur**

▸ *WB p. 49*

1 Yoyo, a special cafe in Glasgow, Scotland

The Yoyo Youth Cafe is in Glasgow's city centre, but young people come to it from all over the city. The service is open 52 weeks of the year, 7 days a week. Many young people come to have a chat with friends. We offer free access to the internet and there is a coffee bar where you can buy inexpensive hot food, snacks and drinks.

In addition, we offer special services. Our *Drop In* service, for example, is for young people aged 12–21 who want to talk about something important in their lives. It might be a problem at school, or maybe they are in trouble with the police. Sometimes it's a problem in the family, or on the internet. At our *Drop In*, everybody can talk with a youth worker or social worker who will listen and discuss what they can do. More than 50,000 young people have used this service in the past ten years. The *Drop In* times are from 3 p.m. to 9 p.m. on Mondays and Wednesdays and 4 p.m. to 10.30 p.m. on Fridays.

We know that families can have good days and bad days. So we also offer a friendly Family Cafe where families can have a break from daily life and chill out. Our friendly workers are here to listen and help you find information. There are fun activities for all the family if you wish to join in. But it's OK if you just want to sit and buy a snack or a drink. The Family Cafe is open from 10 a.m. to 4.30 p.m. on Saturdays and Sundays.

We have special projects which try to help people deal with problems in their lives. For example, our Anti-Violence[1] project discusses violence. Many young people see violence in the home or on the street. We understand that many young people who see violence do not know what to do. And we understand that they are often frightened. We discuss how people can help a friend, or when people should go to the police. Our project helps people to lead safer lives in the future.

Find the right place in the article then read it *carefully*!
eg: <u>in</u>expensive hot food = <u>not</u> expensive

Read the text and then decide if sentences 1–8 are true or false. Tick (✓) the right box.

	true	false
1 The cafe isn't open every day of the week.		
2 Young people can eat and drink without paying a lot of money.		
3 It is only for people who want to talk about their problems.		
4 Young people can talk about all sorts of different problems.		
5 You can play games at the Family Cafe.		
6 The Family Cafe is open on Saturday evenings.		
7 The people at Yoyo know that people who have seen violence are often scared.		
8 The police come to Yoyo to help people.		

[1] anti-violence *gegen Gewalt*

2 Four English students are in a town in Germany

20

You will hear a group of four English students. They are in a German town for the first time. Listen and complete the sentences.

Get ready! Read the sentences before you listen. Then you'll know what information you need.

1 The English students like the cafes because

a) they're cheap ☐ b) people sit outside ☐ c) the cakes are good ☐ d) they're empty ☐.

2 They are surprised when they come out of the butchers' shop because they have

a) no sausages ☐ b) 4 sausages ☐ c) 8 sausages ☐ d) the wrong sausage ☐.

3 Josh wants to cross the road because he wants to buy

a) fruit ☐ b) chicken ☐ c) drinks ☐ d) bread ☐.

4 There is nearly an accident because Josh didn't see

a) a bus ☐ b) a taxi ☐ c) a car ☐ d) the red light ☐.

5 The students are surprised at the traffic lights because nobody

a) talks ☐ b) waits ☐ c) looks at them ☐ d) crosses the road ☐.

6 A scoop of ice cream costs

a) € 1 ☐ b) € 1.50 ☐ c) € 2 ☐ d) € 2.50 ☐.

3 A picture of London

Look at the picture. Then tell your partner about it. Describe the picture. What is happening? What do you think will happen soon? Do you like the picture? Why (not)? Would you like to visit London? Why (not)?

Remember to use phrases like *on the left, in the background*.

Unit 1

1 What happened last week

1 My friend Tom was ill last Tuesday and he *stayed* at home *so* in the evening I *phoned* him.

2 On Wednesday after school I *went* to his house *and* we *talked* about TV programmes and *listened* to music.

3 On Thursday Tom was better *so* he *came* to school again.

4 On Friday I was ill and I *didn't go* to school. I was sad *because* Tom *didn't phone* me.

3 Next weekend

a)

1 On Saturday morning it'll be *rainy.*

2 On Saturday afternoon *it'll be sunny.*

3 On *Sunday morning it'll be windy.*

4 *On Sunday afternoon it'll be cloudy and hot.*

b)

We*'ll take a tent, sleeping bags, a map, pullovers and rain jackets.*

Unit 2

1 Your body

1 head
2 *nose*
3 *throat*
4 *mouth*

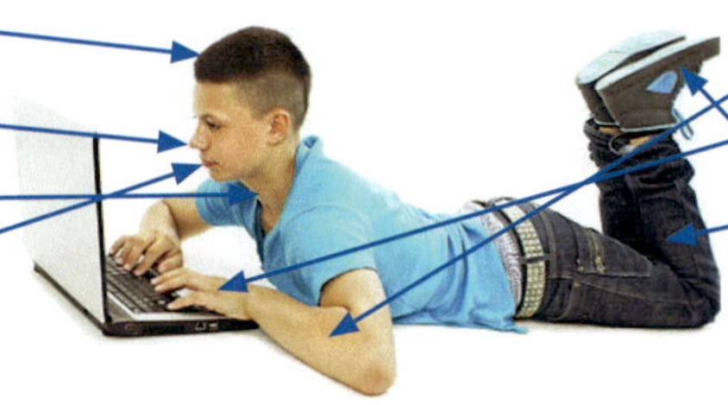

5 *arm*
6 *hand*
7 *leg*
8 *foot*

2 At the farm park

1 Dogs *shouldn't* go into the farm park.

2 Parents *have to* be with their children.

3 Are you hungry? You *should* go to Adam's Kitchen.

4 You *don't have to / can* use the barbecues.

5 You can wear special clothes to the Halloween party but you *don't have to.*

Unit 3

1 Transport words

1 plane	airport
2 ferry	harbour
3 bus	bus stop
4 Tube train	station
5 car	garage

2 Places in the High Street

Unit 4

1 Next weekend

a)

1 Do you make porridge *with milk and sugar?*

2 Are they the scones that *you eat with jam and cream?*

3 What is *black pudding? And what are kippers?*

b)

1 Der Haferbrei wird mit *Salz und Wasser gemacht.*

2 Potato scones isst man mit *Käse, Ei oder Wurst.*

3 Black pudding ist *Blutwurst – nicht süß* – und Kipper ist *Fisch.*

2 Now write about your hiking trip

Mum and I *had* three days in the Highlands. On the first day we *went* hiking in the mountains. It was cold, so we *wore* warm clothes. We *packed* lots of food and *took* a good map. We *wanted* to climb Ben Nevis, Scotland's highest mountain. It's only 1,344 metres high, but we *didn't get* to the top, because it *started* to snow! I *didn't know* the weather was like that in Scotland. We *came* back down the mountain and *ate* our food in the car.

LF 1 REVISION Simple present

bejahte Sätze Yes

I You We They	start early.
He She It	starts early.

Mit dem *simple present* (einfache Gegenwart) sagst du, was oft oder jeden Tag passiert und auch was selten oder nie geschieht:
I often go to the sports club.
We never have lunch at school.

verneinte Sätze No

I You We They	don't start early.
He She It	doesn't start early.

Fragen mit do/does ?

Do I Do you Does he / she / it Do we Do they	like crabs?

He doesn't like dogs.

Fragen mit Fragewörtern ?

Where do I go now?
Why do you do this?
What does he / she / it do?
When do we arrive?
How do they run?

LF 2 REVISION Present progressive

I'm reading a comic.
Ich lese gerade einen Comic.

Dad is cooking dinner.
Papa macht gerade das Abendessen.

What are you doing at the moment?
Was machst du jetzt gerade?

Mit dem *present progressive* (*ing*-Form) sagst du, was gerade jetzt passiert.
Damit beschreibst du auch, was man auf Bildern tut.

Diese Zeitangaben findest du oft in Sätzen im *present progressive:*
now, at the moment, today.

bejahte Sätze Yes

I'm You're He's She's It's We're You're They're	helping.

verneinte Sätze No

I'm not You aren't He isn't She isn't It isn't We aren't You aren't They aren't	helping.

Fragen ?

Am I Are you Is he Is she Is it Are we Are you Are they	helping?

LF 3 REVISION Simple past

Yesterday evening I watched TV.
Gestern Abend habe ich ferngesehen/sah ich fern.

Last week I didn't go to football training
Letzte Woche ging ich nicht zum Fußballtraining.

Did you watch the fireworks last night?
Hast du gestern abend das Feuerwerk gesehen?

Mit dem *simple past* sprichst du über Dinge, die in der Vergangenheit geschehen sind. Du verwendest es oft mit Zeitangaben wie ***yesterday, last week, last year, last summer, in 2010.***

bejahte Sätze Yes

I You He/She/It We They	helped.

verneinte Sätze No

I You He/She/It We They	didn't help.

Fragen mit did ?

Did	I you he/she/it we they	help?

Fragen mit Fragewörtern ?

What	did	she	watch?
When	did	it	finish?
Where	did	they	go?

What did she watch?
– She watched the fireworks.

LF 4 Present perfect

I have moved house three times.
Ich bin schon dreimal umgezogen.

My little sister has never been on a plane.
Meine kleine Schwester ist noch nie geflogen.

Have you ever ridden a pony?
Bist du schon einmal geritten?

Mit dem *present perfect* sagst du, dass du etwas schon einmal, öfter oder noch nie gemacht hast.
Du verwendest es oft mit Zeitangaben wie ***ever, never, once, twice, lots of times.***

bejahte Sätze Yes

I You We They	have started early. ('ve started)
He She It	has started early.

verneinte Sätze No

I You We They	haven't started early.
He She It	hasn't started early.

Fragen und Kurzantworten ?

Have you started?	– Yes, I have. – No, I haven't.
Has she started?	– Yes, she has. – No, she hasn't.

Jacob has worked a lot today.

LF 5 REVISION *Will*-future

Wenn du vermutest, was in der Zukunft geschehen könnte, verwendest du das ***will-future.***
Die Sätze beginnen oft mit ***I think, maybe, I'm sure*** oder ***I hope.***

I think you'll have a great birthday party.
Ich glaube, du wirst eine tolle Geburtstagsparty haben.

Maybe we'll have a barbecue in the garden.
Vielleicht grillen wir im Garten.

I'm sure the weather will be nice.
Ich bin sicher, das Wetter wird schön sein.

bejahte Sätze Yes

It	will 'll	be sunny tomorrow.

verneinte Sätze No

It	will not won't	be sunny tomorrow.

Fragen und Kurzantworten ?

Will it be sunny tomorrow? – Yes, it will.
– No, it won't.

LF 6 REVISION *Going to*-future

Mit ***going to …*** sagst du
– was du vorhast oder für die Zukunft geplant hast,
– was wahrscheinlich bald passieren wird.

We're going to have a picnic on Sunday.
Wir haben vor, am Sonntag ein Picknick zu machen.

Oh no, he's going to fall!
Oh nein, er fällt gleich herunter!

bejahte Sätze Yes

I'm You're He's/She's We're They're	going to	watch TV.

verneinte Sätze No

I'm not You're not He's/She's not We're not They're not	going to	watch TV.

LF 7 *Have to/can/should*

Mit ***can/can't*** sagst du, was jemand (nicht) tun kann oder darf.

Can

I can play the guitar.
Tom can't go to school today – he's ill.
Can I open the window?

Mit ***should/shouldn't*** rätst du jemandem, etwas zu tun, oder nicht zu tun.

Should

You should take your pullover – it's cold.
She shouldn't eat so much chocolate.

Mit ***have to*** sagst du, was jemand tun muss.
Mit ***don't have to*** sagst du, was jemand nicht zu tun braucht.

Have to

I have to help me in the kitchen now.
He has to look after his sister today.
You don't have to eat this.
She doesn't have to do chores.

LF 8 Reflexivpronomen

It was my mistake so I blame myself.
Es war mein Fehler, also gebe ich mir die Schuld.

He has cut himself.
Er hat sich geschnitten.

We can look after ourselves.
Wir können uns um uns selbst kümmern.

I wash myself.
You wash yourself.
He washes himself.
She washes herself.
We wash ourselves.
You wash yourselves.
They wash themselves.

WORDBANK

alarm clock

blanket

charger

coffee machine

cup

curtain

headphones

knife

matches

mirror

pan

plate

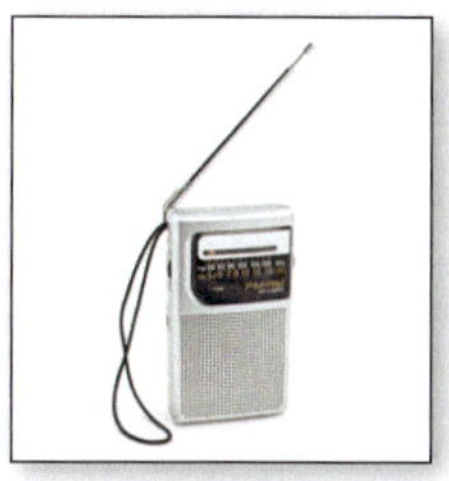
radio

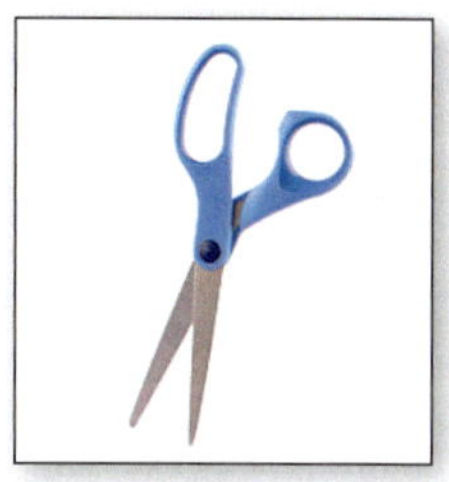
scissors

shampoo

soap

spoon

suitcase

toothbrush

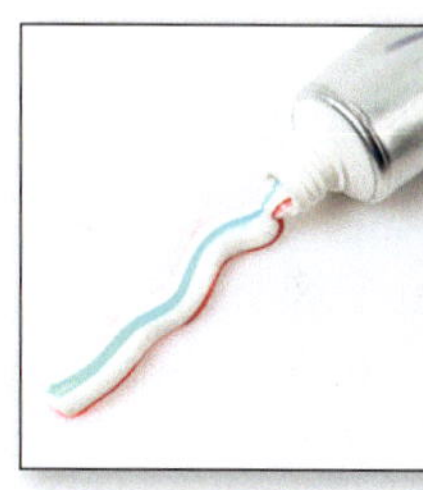
toothpaste

torch

towel

umbrella

washing machine

▸ *WB p. 50–51*

Illustrationen

Beehive Illustration, Cirencester (S.47: Pete Smith); **Kate Davies**, Colerne (S.6; S.15 oben; S.19 oben; S.20 unten; S.26 mi-li; S.28 unten; S.32; S.57); **Katrin Inzinger**, Berlin (S.9; S.14; S.15 unten; S.21; S.24; S.29; S.40; S.50–51; S.59)

Bildquellen

Action Press, Hamburg (S.5.2); **F1 Online**, Frankfurt (S.5.6); **Corbis**, Düsseldorf (S.8A: alecmoses MOSES/ Demotix; S.10 li (WildCountry); **Cornelsen Schulverlage**, Berlin (S.41.6; S.45 unten); **Fotolia**, New York (S.31 o-li & S.37 oben: Farina3000); **GlowImages**, München (S.5.3: Robert Harding; S.8B: Steve Vidler); **Interfoto**, München (S.27: Writers Pictures Ltd: Facundo Arrizabalaga); **Mauritius Images**, Mittenwald (S.5.4: Steve Vidler; S.7 market: Alamy; S.12: Alamy; S.28: Alamy; S.33 oben (beide): Alamy; S.34: Alamy); **Shutterstock**, New York (S.3 oben: Dimec, Thames: Michaelpuche, Big Ben: Byjeng, unten: David Fowler; S.5.1: Elena Elisseeva, 5: Alan Jeffrey; S.7 oben: Julia Zakharova; S.8C Magdanatka, D: Samuel Micut; S.10 re: Anastasia Kucherenko; S.12 David Noble; S.18 & 54 li: Nelson Marques, re: Alex Kalmbach, unten: Javier Brosch; S.19 unten: Bobkeenan Photography; S.20 li: Max Topchii, re: Innershadows Photography; S.22: jordache; S.23: pavalena; S.26 oben: Jeka; mittig: Matthew Dixon, re: Lena Pantiukh; S.31 re: east; A: Luis Molinero, B: draganica, C: Anton Chalakov, D: oksana2010, E : Olesia Bilkei, F: margouillat photo; S.33 unten: infografick; S.36: Roman Sotola; S.37 unten: Steve Collender; S.40 & 59: Holger Graebner; S.41.1: astudio, 2 Mike Heywood, 3: neila, 4: Stockcube, 5: Bill McKelvie; S.42 o-li: Mat Hayward, o-re: Stuart Monk, u-li: TracyWhiteside, u-re: Jorg Hackemann; S.43 Haus: Ksusha Dusmikeeva, Burg: Dmitry Naumov; S.44: rui vale souse; S.45 & 55 oben: Alan Uster; S.47 mittig: Rob Byron, unten: snowturtle; S.48 re: Andrew Sproule, li: Robert Neumann; S.50 & 63 Würfel: Mexrix, Tasse: Odua Images, Teller: BorisShevchuk, Kochtopf: Alaettin YILDIRIM, Messer: pukach, Waschmaschine: g215, Koffer: iko, Wecker: lendy16, Radio: Marcio Jose Bastos Silva; S.51 & 63 Kopfhörer: Maximus256, Decke: Nordling, Vorhang: K. Miri Photography, Seife: Zocha_K, Zahnbürste: Nikola Spasenoski, Handtuch: Gilmanshin, Zahnpaste: dcb, Regenschirm: Africa Studio, Taschenlampe: zirconicusso, Spiegel: Cherkas, Streichhölzer: slavchovr, Ladegerät: Rfarrarons, Kaffeemaschine: Alexandru Nika, Löffel: Nixx Photography, Schere: Jason Swalwell, Shampooflasche: mihalec, Haare waschen: altafulla; S.53: Maaster; S.56 unten: Monkey Business Images; S.58: Jeka; S.60: Ron Leishman; S.61: Rudie Strummer; S.62: Igor Zakowski); **Vario Images**, Bonn (S.56 oben: Cultura); **Peter Wirtz**, Dormagen (S.30; S.35)

Titelbild

Shutterstock.com / Bernhard Richter

Deine **Audios** findest du hier:

1. Gehe auf scook.de.
2. Gib den unten stehenden Zugangscode in die Box ein.
3. Hab viel Spaß mit den Audios.

Dein Zugangscode auf
www.scook.de | yn76c-4bmrq